SESAME STREET 123

Being THANKFUL with Gabrielle

A Book about Gratitude

Marie-Therese Miller

Lerner Publications ◆ Minneapolis

Sesame Street's mission has always been about teaching kids much more than simply the ABCs and 123s. This series of books about nurturing the positive character traits of mindfulness, gratitude, self-confidence, and responsibility will help children grow into the best versions of themselves. So come along with your funny, furry friends from Sesame Street as they learn about making themselves—and the world—smarter, stronger, and kinder.

—Sincerely, the Editors at Sesame Street

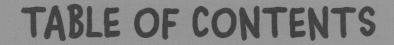

TABLE OF CONTENTS

What Is Thankfulness?

Being thankful means we are grateful.

I am thankful for music so I can sing and dance!

Being grateful is feeling happy for the good things in our lives.

Showing Gratitude

We are grateful for our families.

I am grateful for my dad. He cheers for me at my soccer games.

They love us and take care of us.

We are grateful
for our friends.

It's fun to play together!

Who are you grateful for?

9

I am thankful for my librarian. He helps me find good books to read!

Firefighters keep us safe. Doctors and nurses help us feel better.

We are grateful for sunny days.

What's your favorite thing to do on a sunny day?

It's fun to swing and climb on the jungle gym.

We are thankful for rainy days too.

I am grateful for rain. It helps my flowers grow!

We can splash in puddles. Sometimes we see a rainbow!

We are grateful for our food.

Crunchy broccoli and bananas taste delicious.

My mom and I are thankful for carrots that we grow in our garden.

We are grateful
for quiet times.

Listening to a bedtime story or hugging a teddy bear helps us feel calm.

What do you do during your quiet time?

I am grateful for you!

There are so many things to be thankful for. What are you grateful for?

BE A BUDDY!

Who are you grateful to have in your life? Draw a picture of something fun you do together. Give the picture to that person as a thank-you.

Glossary

community: a group of people living in a certain area

delicious: when something tastes good

firefighters: people who are trained to put out fires

gratitude: being thankful

Read More

Miller, Marie-Therese. *Caring with Bert and Ernie: A Book about Empathy*. Minneapolis: Lerner Publications, 2021.

Riehecky, Janet. *Thank You*. Mankato, MN: Child's World, 2022.

Shulman, Naomi. *Give Thanks: You Can Reach Out and Spread Joy!* North Adams, MA: Storey, 2021.

Index

Photo Acknowledgments

Image credits: jacoblund/iStock/Getty Images, p. 4; Jose Luis Pelaez Inc/DigitalVision/Getty Images, pp. 5, 7; kali9/E+/Getty Images, p. 6; Ariel Skelley/DigitalVision/Getty Images, p. 8; JW LTD/Stone/Getty Images, p. 9; Adene Sanchez/E+/Getty Images, p. 10; SDI Productions/E+/Getty Images, p. 11; Tang Ming Tung/Stone/Getty Images, p. 12; Nitat Termmee/Moment/Getty Images, p. 13; NickyLloyd/E+/Getty Images, p. 14; ArtMarie/E+/Getty Images, p. 15; RyanJLane/E+/Getty Images, p. 16; JGI/Jamie Grill/Tetra images/Getty Images, p. 18; PeopleImages/iStock/Getty Images, p. 19; Jasper Cole/Tetra images/Getty Images, p. 20.

I am grateful for John, Meghan, John Vincent, Erin, Elizabeth, Michelle, and Greyson

Lerner Publications Company
An imprint of Lerner Publishing Group, Inc.
241 First Avenue North
Minneapolis, MN 55401 USA

For reading levels and more information, look up this title at www.lernerbooks.com.

Main body text set in Billy Infant.
Typeface provided by SparkyType.

Designer: Emily Harris **Photo Editor:** Annie Zheng
Lerner team: Connie Kuhnz

Library of Congress Cataloging-in-Publication Data

Names: Miller, Marie-Therese, author.
Title: Being thankful with Gabrielle : a book about gratitude / Marie-Therese Miller.
Description: Minneapolis : Lerner Publications, [2024] | Series: Sesame Street character guides | Includes bibliographical references and index. | Audience: Ages 4–8 | Audience: Grades K–1 | Summary: "Readers learn with their Sesame Street friends about gratitude. Then they discover all they have to be thankful for from community helpers to the food that gives our bodies fuel"—Provided by publisher.
Identifiers: LCCN 2022037263 (print) | LCCN 2022037264 (ebook) | ISBN 9781728486789 (library binding) | ISBN 9798765600832 (ebook)
Subjects: LCSH: Gratitude in children—Juvenile literature. | Gratitude—Juvenile literature.
Classification: LCC BF575.G68 M55 2024 (print) | LCC BF575.G68 (ebook) | DDC 179/.9—dc23/eng/20221205

LC record available at https://lccn.loc.gov/2022037263
LC ebook record available at https://lccn.loc.gov/2022037264

Manufactured in the United States of America
1-52691-50862-11/21/2022